TRUE CRIME

Spies

John Townsend

Raintree

www.raintreepublishers.co.uk

Visit our website to find out more information about **Raintree** books.

To order:

 Phone 44 (0) 1865 888113

 Send a fax to 44 (0) 1865 314091

Visit the Raintree Bookshop at **www.raintreepublishers.co.uk** to browse our catalogue and order online.

First published in Great Britain by
Raintree, Halley Court, Jordan Hill, Oxford OX2 8EJ,
part of Harcourt Education.
Raintree is a registered trademark of Harcourt
Education Ltd.

© Harcourt Education Ltd 2006
First published in paperback in 2007

Editorial: Melanie Copland and Sarah Chappelow
Design: Lucy Owen and Kamae Design
Picture Research: Hannah Taylor and Ginny Stroud-Lewis
Production: Duncan Gilbert

Originated by Repro Multi Warna
Printed and bound in China
by South China Printing Company

10 digit ISBN 1 844 43810 4 (hardback)
13 digit ISBN 978 1844 43810 5 (hardback)
11 10 09 08 07 06
10 9 8 7 6 5 4 3 2 1

10 digit ISBN 1 844 43816 3 (paperback)
13 digit ISBN 978 1844 43816 7 (paperback)
12 11 10 09 08 07
10 9 8 7 6 5 4 3 2 1

British Library Cataloguing in Publication Data
Townsend, John
Spies – (True Crime)
364.1'31
A full catalogue record for this book is available from
the British Library.

Acknowledgements
Alamy Images pp. **title** (Goodshoot), 4–5 (Goodshoot),
5 top (archivberlin Fotoagentur GmbH), 5 bottom
(Ace Stock Limited), 10 (Justin Kase), 13 (archivberlin
Fotoagentur GmbH), 15 (Brand X Pictures), 32–33
(Sebastien Baussais), 35 (Ace Stock Limited), 36 (Zak
Waters), 42 (Leslie Garland Picture Library); Corbis
pp. 4, 5 (Peter Turnley), 6–7, 7 (Arte & Immagini srl),
9 (Tim Wright), 11 (Roger Ressmeyer), 14 (Bettmann),
15 (Tim Graham), 16–17, 20 (Jose Luis Pelaez, Inc.),
21 (Peter Turnley), 22–23, 24 (Stephanie Maze), 26
(Bettmann), 27 right (Bettmann), 27 left (Bettmann),
32, 33 (Downing Larry), 36 (Bettmann), 37 (E O
Hoppe), 42–43 (Reuters); Getty Images pp. 6
(Photodisc), 8 (Photodisc), 8–9, 11 (Time & Life
Pictures), 16 (Photodisc), 18–19 (Photodisc), 22
(Hulton Archive), 25 (Hulton Archive), 28, 34 (Hulton
Archive), 44–45 (Photodisc); Harcourt Education Ltd
p. 19 (Ginny Stroud-Lewis); PA Photos p. 17; Science
Photo Library pp. 30 (Gusto), 35 (Tek Image), 43
(Michael Donne); The Kobal Collection pp. 12
(Danjaq/EON/UA), 29, 30–31 (Paramount/Boland,
Jasin), 37 (Danjaq/EON/UA/Ray Hearne), 38
(Columbia/Famous Artists), 38–39
(MGM/EON/Hamshere, Keith), 41 (Miramax /Ricco
Torres), 40 (Paramount).

Cover photograph of a spy looking through a filing
cabinet reproduced with permission of Corbis/Rich
Eagle.

Every effort has been made to contact copyright
holders of any material reproduced in this book.
Any omissions will be rectified in subsequent
printings if notice is given to the publishers.

The paper used to print this book comes from
sustainable resources.

Contents

Any words appearing in the text in bold, **like this,** are explained in the Glossary. You can also look out for them in the Word Bank at the bottom of each page.

Selling secrets

Getting caught

Anyone caught spying on a country's secrets can expect to be locked away ... or worse!

Spying is a serious crime.

Some old sayings are still very true. One is "curiosity killed the cat". After all, if you go snooping about, you can get into big trouble. Snooping about is also called spying. It can be risky. Every spy risks getting into danger, as well as ending up in prison for a long time. The golden rule for any spy is very simple: never get caught. As soon as someone finds out who you really are, it is all over. The game is up. The secret to spying is to stay secret.

The penalty for espionage	
UK, Canada, New Zealand	prison sentence up to 14 years
Australia	prison sentence up to 25 years
USA	maximum penalty is the death sentence

Word Bank   espionage spying to get secret information

Espionage!

Spying is about finding information to steal. Stealing secrets is a crime. If you try to find out someone's bank details without permission, or if you copy the plans for a country's weapons, you are spying. Spying is also called **espionage**. Espionage can lead to prison ... or worse.

Most countries use spies to find out about other countries. This is called **intelligence** gathering. Spies who do this are called secret agents. You never know who they might be. Some spies work for their government. Other spies sell secrets to anyone who will pay. A few do both.

Find out later...

When is a mole a spy?

Why do spies have their eyes on Coca-Cola™?

What secrets can teeth hold?

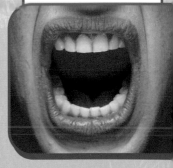

You never know when you are being spied on.

intelligence secret information gathered by spies, which tells one country what another is doing

Long ago

The ancient Egyptians, who built the pyramids about 4000 years ago, had an army of spies. This "secret service" is mentioned in some of the writings they left behind. The spies kept an eye on their neighbours. It was important to be ready if an enemy was planning to attack.

Spying can be like a game of chess. Each move must be well planned. But the risk of losing can be deadly with spying.

More than a game

During a test, a cheat might try to look at your answers. So you might let them copy a lot of wrong answers!

Letting a spy find out just what you want them to can be a clever trick. Another trick is if the spy takes the false information and pretends to believe it. Spying can be a confusing business.

Word Bank   civil war when soldiers from the same country fight against each other

In the beginning...

People have always spied on others. Even the first humans, who lived in caves, sent out spies to check out their enemies before going off to attack them. It has been the same with armies ever since. Success in war often depends on surprising the enemy. That is why good **intelligence** matters.

In the 1860s, the two armies in the American **Civil War** used spies. Men and women joined enemy camps to find out what was going on behind enemy lines. Once they knew the plans, they would have to get the information back to their own side. It was a risky business.

Spies warned Queen Elizabeth I that Spanish ships were on the way.

The Spanish are coming ...

Spying was big business in England in the 1500s. Francis Walsingham worked for Queen Elizabeth I of England as her **spymaster**. He sent secret agents all over Europe, who informed him of any threats. When the Spanish Armada came to attack England in 1588, the English were ready. The spies had done a good job.

Spying helped soldiers in the American Civil War.

Heroes or criminals?

People have different ideas about spying. If spies are on our side and working for us, we see them as brave. If they are sending back our secrets to the enemy, we see them as **traitors**. All through history, traitors were killed in cruel ways. They were hated. In wartime many spies were shot for **treason**.

Even today, spies sometimes keep a poison pill with them. If they get caught, they swallow it quickly. If not, they know that all kinds of **torture** will be used to make them talk. They will be forced to tell what secrets they know. Many prefer to die rather than face the torture.

Paying the price

The Tower of London (above) was a high security prison for hundreds of years. Many criminals were tortured there. That included spies – even in the last 100 years. During the First World War, eleven spies were kept there before they were **executed**.

Soldiers often receive information gathered by spies to help them fight a battle.

Word Bank

executed put to death for breaking the law
traitor someone who betrays a person or country

Punishment

There are clear rules today for anyone who passes US secrets to another country. This is a shortened part of the United States's law about espionage:

" Any person who sets out to harm the United States by passing any document* to any foreign country shall be punished. Any person found guilty of an offence that concerns nuclear weapons, military spacecraft, early warning systems, or other major weapons system, shall be punished by death. "

*A document might be a code book, signal book, sketch, photograph, plan, map, model, note, or instrument.

A spy could be strapped to a chair and shot.

---

treason crime of harming your country, or of helping its enemies during war
torture causing great physical and /or mental pain to get information

Keeping secrets

In the last 100 years, the world of spying has grown bigger than ever before. **Espionage** has become very well organized. By 2000, thousands of people were working in the intelligence services around the world. Countries now spend millions of pounds each day trying to protect their secrets. They spend millions more trying to discover everyone else's.

For well over 50 years the **CIA** has been gathering **intelligence** for the United States. It has spies in countries all around the world. The other US crime organization working in espionage is the **FBI**. It protects government secrets and catches enemy spies. Much of its work is top secret.

MI5 and MI6

The UK's Security Service is **MI5**. That stands for 'Military Intelligence unit 5'. It has dealt with threats to the country's security since 1916. **MI6** gathers intelligence from other countries and its proper name is the Secret Intelligence Service.

MI6 headquarters in London.

SSHSH – it's a secret

The number of staff working for the CIA is secret. It is probably about 16,000 people. The FBI has almost 11,500 special agents.

Word Bank   CIA Central Intelligence Agency of the United States
FBI United States's Federal Bureau of Investigation

The Cold War

After the end of the Second World War in 1945, spies might have thought there would be fewer secrets to worry about. The world was at peace. But the next 40 years were busier for spies than ever before. This time of **mistrust** between many countries was known as the Cold War. The **USSR** and the United States became enemies, but there was no actual fighting between them. Spies were hard at work. They had to find out what **nuclear** weapons were being made and where they were hidden. The CIA and **KGB** had spies everywhere.

The KGB

Russia's secret service is called the **KGB**. It had thousands of spies all around the world. They found out many of the USA's secrets. In 2000, 10 years after the end of the Cold War, Italy named spies who worked for Russia. Over 250 Italians had been paid by the KGB to spy for them.

The CIA gathers secrets for the US government.

The headquarters of the KGB in Russia.

CIA Operations Center

---

mistrust having no trust in someone
USSR Union of Soviet Socialist Republics – now called Russia

Why spy?

A good spy is...

- A good actor – you must appear to be what you are not.
- Cool and calm under pressure – you must keep your nerve.
- Tough – you must be prepared to **betray** anyone, even your friends.
- Careful – especially in what you say.
- Good at keeping secrets – even under **torture**.
- Good at speaking different languages.

Do you think real-life spies are like the baddies in James Bond films?

> " Your mission is to join the enemy. You are to become one of them. Gain their trust. Tell to us all you discover. If you are found out, we will deny we know you. You are on your own. "

Would you want a job like this? Why do some people become spies when there are so many risks? Is it because they need danger and excitement? Perhaps there are other reasons. In a war, spies can help their country win or lose. At such times, it is easier to see why people might want to work for their country as a spy. What about at other times?

Word Bank

betray to act against your friend or country
informer person who tells information

For your country

Some people love their country and want to serve it however they can. They are prepared to risk spying. Other people have strong **political** views. They may feel so strongly that they want to harm countries or organizations with opposite views. By joining the "enemy" they can damage it from the inside.

Members of the police sometimes join criminal gangs to become **informers**. Although these spies act as gang members, they report back to the police all that is going on. These gangs might be drug gangs or terrorist groups. It is very dangerous work, but it usually ends with the criminals being arrested.

Moles

A mole is a small animal that lives under ground out of sight. It is also the name given to some spies. A mole is a spy who works **undercover**, deep inside an organization. They "lie low" for a long time to gain trust. They dig out information and report it back secretly.

Not all moles are as harmless as this one!

political beliefs about power and how to organize society
undercover acting in secret inside an organization

Everyday spies

Some people cannot help acting like spies! They are always watching what is going on in their neighbourhoods. This can often be a good thing in keeping a lookout for crime. But some neighbours watch too much. They want to know everyone's private business. It can be more than just being nosy. Some people use telescopes or cameras to find out more. It can be a crime if they take their spying too far and **invade** another person's **privacy**.

I know where you live

Many famous film stars know what it is like to be spied on or followed. But sometimes fans do more. They become **stalkers**. They want to know every tiny detail of the star's life. Some stars have even reported stalkers going through their rubbish bins to find out what shampoo they use!

Stalking does not just happen to stars. Many people report being spied on day and night. Stalkers who threaten people are usually sent to prison. Maybe more than you think…

" About 1.4 million people are stalked every year in the United States. That is 1 in 45 men and 1 in 12 women being stalked at some time in their lives. "

(National Centre for Victims of Crime)

Peeping Tom was the only one to see Lady Godiva.

Did you know?
The name Peeping Tom is given to someone who spies on people through little holes like keyholes. The name is said to come from a tailor called Tom who lived in Coventry, England in the 11th century. He was the only person to watch when a famous woman rode by naked! Her name was Lady Godiva.

Word Bank

invade disturb or move in on
privacy freedom from being disturbed or watched

Stalkers can make their victims' lives a misery.

Spying on Royals

Prince William is said to have over 200 stalkers. A team of **psychiatrists** is on 24-hour call to deal with any who become real threats. They advise royal bodyguards on how to deal with stalkers who become far more than just fans.

psychiatrist doctor who deals with the mind, feelings, and behaviour
stalker someone who watches and follows other people

15

Snooping for a living

Some jobs involve a lot of spying. That often means snooping, hiding, and watching. Private investigators have to gather all kinds of information. That could mean **phone tapping** or secretly setting up **surveillance** equipment. They often have to search for evidence, but they should not break the law to do it.

Anyone can hire a "private eye" to investigate **legally**. If you are the manager of a shop and you think one of your staff is taking money from the till, what do you do? You could employ a spy to catch them at it!

Could you tell if your phone was bugged?

Bugged?

Some people think their telephone might be bugged. They try a test by phoning someone they trust. They have already decided what to say – usually a made-up piece of gossip. Then they wait. If the story gets out into the open, they know someone has been listening. There must be a spy about!

Prison officers watch out for trouble.

Word Bank   expose show or tell everyone
legally allowed by law

Journalists

Some news reporters like to **expose** criminals at work. That could involve setting up a secret camera to film a **con artist** working. Or it might mean spying on people by secretly recording them committing crimes.

Ted Conover, a New York journalist, wanted to find out about prison life. But prisons would not let him in to investigate. So he became a prison officer for 10 months in 1997. New York has thousands of prisoners and Conover wanted to find out how they were treated by the prison officers. The only way was to become a spy. Only then could he write his book truthfully.

Spying on the police

Mark Daly spent months in 2003 training to be a police officer in Manchester, UK. The other police officers being trained had no idea he was really an **undercover** journalist. Daly was trying to expose racism in the police force. He secretly filmed some racist conversations. This led to big changes in the way police officers are chosen.

Mark Daly won an award for uncovering racism in the UK police force.

phone tapping listening in on a telephone phone call
surveillance watching closely

Cyber spies

Computers have opened up a whole new world for spies. Huge amounts of secret information is stored on computers round the world. A lot of people would like to break into computers to see this information. A clever **hacker** can do just that and leave no trace that a crime has been committed. A cyber spy does not even have to leave home.

Experts are always making better software to protect computers. Even so, cyber spies keep breaking through to look at information. Some do far more. They steal information or destroy files. Cyber **espionage** is a growing crime.

Student charged with hacking to give herself top grades (2002)

A student from Delaware, USA, broke into her school's computer system and gave herself three "grade A" marks, police said. The student is charged with identity theft and illegal access to a computer system. She used a teacher's password to do a little spying and adjusting.

Cyber spies use computers.

Word Bank   hacker someone skilled with computers who breaks security

Keeping an eye on you

Someone could be spying on you every time you use a computer. Every mouse click, every e-mail sent, and every word typed or deleted can be recorded. The latest software tells all your details to the person spying on you. That could be the police, your teachers, or anyone else. Each morning, thousands of bosses are able to check up on what their staff did at work the day before. They can find out if anyone played games, shopped online, or looked at websites They can see all the "conversations" that went on in chat rooms, too. So computers may not be as private as you might think!

Being watched

Some governments keep a very close eye on what people use computers for. China may have up to 40,000 Internet police to check what people are doing online. Some Internet cafes in Beijing have cameras looking at computer screens to record what users are up to.

Are you being watched?

Spies at work

Imagine you were the boss of a business and another company was doing better than you. You could try to find out their latest plans. Then you could beat them. Or you could try to find a list of all their customers. Then you could get them all to switch to your business. But stealing information from **rivals** is a crime, and you would be guilty of industrial **espionage**.

Spies can lose companies a lot of money.

Word Bank

rival enemy or competitor
rumour story that may not be true

It's the real thing

The recipe for the flavour of Coca-Cola™ is a huge secret. Just imagine if another company got hold of the recipe! Many spies have tried. It is said the top-secret recipe is locked inside a safe, in a **vault** at the Trust Company of Georgia, USA. Only the company bosses can allow the vault to be opened. Many rivals have tried to find the secret to Coca Cola's™ success. So far it remains a mystery.

There is a **rumour** that no one at Coca-Cola™ knows the full recipe. The bosses only know half each. This means the recipe will stay a secret even if a spy tries to make one of them talk!

Not many people know this...

(Apart from a few spies, of course)

- People in Mexico and Iceland drink the most Coca-Cola™ per person.
- Coca-Cola™ in Chinese means, "To make mouth happy".
- Every second over 7000 Coca-Colas™ are drunk around the world.

Coca-Cola™ have a very big secret to protect from spies.

Famous spies

Did you know?

From 1914 to 1918, 70 million men and women served in the First World War. Many were spies. But so were thousands of pigeons. Armies had to send secret messages quickly, and they did not have mobile phones or radios. Messages were tied to pigeons' legs and off they flew, back to base.

Most of the spies we know about from the past got into the job because of war.

First World War spies

Mata Hari was a famous Dutch dancer. She knew many important people across Europe. When the First World War started, the Germans asked her to spy for them as she had so many foreign **contacts**. She agreed to send messages in a secret code from France to Germany. The French found one of her messages and managed to crack the code. They arrested Mata Hari as a spy. She was found guilty and shot in 1917 at the age of 41.

Word Bank   contact someone you know who has important information in business or government

The flying hero

Near the end of the war, in October 1918, over 200 US soldiers were surrounded by German troops in France. They were trapped and needed help. The only way to get a message out was to release a spy pigeon called Cher Ami and hope he made it to the army headquarters. He flew off with an **SOS** message and a map showing where the men were stuck. He flew 40 kilometres (25 miles) in under half an hour, getting shot in the chest. But he made it back to base and delivered the message. All the soldiers were rescued. Cher Ami was given a medal as the spy pigeon that saved over 200 men.

Don't shoot our spies!

Killing homing pigeons can result in 6 Months Imprisonment or £100 Fine.

The public are reminded that homing pigeons are doing valuable work.

£5 reward will be paid by the National Homing Union for information leading to the conviction of any person **SHOOTING HOMING PIGEONS.**

Information should be given to the Police, Military Post or to the Secretary of the Union, C C Plackett, 14, East Parade, Leeds, UK

Spy pigeons had to be kept safe.

Spy pigeons were kept in trailers like this during the First World War.

Women spies

Some of the bravest spies in wartime have been women. Some were so keen to support the soldiers that they offered to work behind enemy lines, where there was great danger. In the Second World War women spies often dressed as **peasants**. It was thought the enemy would never think a peasant woman could be a spy.

An innocent old woman – or a master spy?

Second World War spies

In the Second World War, Germany **invaded** France. Many French people became spies to plot against the German **Nazis**. The spies also set up secret escape routes for UK and US pilots, who had crash landed in France. Virginia Hall from Baltimore, USA went to help them.

The Nazis were soon hunting for Virginia. Although she had a false leg, she managed to escape on foot over the Pyrenees Mountains that separate France and Spain. But she was soon back in France, dressed as an old milkmaid. The Nazis put up a wanted poster – "GET THE WOMAN WITH THE LIMP." So Virginia did her best not to limp! They never found her and she survived the War.

Word Bank   Nazis government in Germany from 1933 to 1945 led by Adolf Hitler

Bravery

Violette Bushell was born in 1921. Her father was English and her mother was French. When the Second World War started she married a French captain. He was soon killed by the Germans, so Violette was set on **revenge**. She offered help to the British Secret Service, as she knew that secret agents in France needed help. As she spoke French, she could help agents spy on the Germans. She parachuted into France and began working as a spy.

After many **missions**, she shot some German soldiers and was caught. In spite of terrible **torture**, she gave nothing away. She was shot as a spy shortly before the war ended.

Many brave men and women such as Violette Bushell helped the war effort.

Air mail

Pigeons helped spies in the Second World War as well as the First World War. The UK Pigeon Service supplied about 200,000 pigeons and the US Army bred 50,000. The Germans used spy pigeons, too. MI5 agents in the UK used hawks to catch enemy German pigeons! Some German pigeons were actually kept as prisoners of war!

---

peasant poor country person who works on the land
revenge get even with someone

Cold War spies

After the Second World War, the United States and **USSR** became **rivals**. They began making bigger weapons to threaten each other with. This was the Cold War. Many people who knew secrets could make easy money by selling information to the other side.

John Walker was in the US Navy in 1967 when he offered to help the **KGB**. Soon his brother, son, and friend joined him in **espionage**. Because of their jobs in the Navy, they could easily get hold of secret documents, codes, and code machines. They dropped them off in secret places where Russian spies were waiting to pick them up – in exchange for plenty of cash.

Julius and Ethel Rosenberg.

Word Bank   convicted prove guilty of a crime
defence to do with a country's military organizations

Greed

John Walker was one of the most damaging spies in US history. The Russians called him their most important spy ever. His job gave him access to many **defence** secrets in the US Navy. He sold them to the Russians over 18 years until he had a big row with his wife. She was so upset that she went to the **FBI** to tell them her husband was a spy. They arrested him in 1985.

It was thought the KGB paid Walker around US $1 million for all those secrets. In court he showed no **regrets** and was even proud of what he had done. He was sent to prison for life.

John Walker (left) during his trial.

Keeping it in the family

John Walker's son, Michael (below), was also sent to prison for spying. He was released 15 years later in 2000, aged 37. His mother never served a prison sentence. Although she had been part of the family spy ring, it was she who ended it with a call to the FBI.

Michael Walker on his way to prison.

regret sadness or disappointment about what has happened

In the news

With the ending of the Cold War in the 1990s, many countries became better friends. That did not mean spying stopped. All countries still have secrets. Where there are secrets, there are always people ready to steal them.

Much of the spying in the 21st century concerns threats from terrorists. Terrorist groups such as **Al-Qaeda** send spies around the world to find information. At the same time, spies are at work from many countries trying to find out where terrorist attacks might happen next. This is very dangerous work.

Double life

A "double agent" is a spy who works for two or more **rival** secret services. You could be pretending to spy for China, but really working for the CIA and spying on the Chinese. How confusing!

Governments need information to stop attacks such as this one in Madrid, Spain.

Word Bank   Al-Qaeda terrorist organization linked with attacks on New York and Washington D.C. on September 11, 2001

Terror suspect held (August 2004)

Abu Eisa al-Hindi was arrested in the UK in August 2004. He was thought to be an Al-Qaeda secret agent. The **CIA** thinks he may also have been to New York to spy on buildings as targets for an attack.

It seems that an Al-Qaeda computer expert arrested in Pakistan was planning an attack on Heathrow airport, London. Files found in his computer also outlined plans for an attack in the United States – where a US$5 million reward had been offered for his capture.

The CIA thinks twelve men arrested in raids across England could be part of a group of Al-Qaeda spies.

US citizen accused of being a Chinese double agent (2004)

Katrina Leung is accused of copying secret US papers. While working as a secret agent for the **FBI**, Mrs Leung was accused of passing secrets to the Chinese. She could face up to 50 years in prison if **convicted**.

Double agents often make spy films very exciting to watch!

Tricks of the trade

Squashing the bugs

A bug transmits radio waves. A special bug **detector** can now find them. Bug detectors lock on to radio waves. They were once huge, but now they fit in one hand. They only work when the bug is switched on. That is why most bugs are remote-controlled – so they can stay switched off most of the time.

What do you need to be a spy? Films often show spies leaping in through windows as they clutch their little case of tricks. So what might they carry in their spy kit?

Bugs

Being able to listen to a secret conversation can give you all kinds of useful information. That is why rooms, cars and phones are sometimes **bugged**. A bug is a small listening device that **transmits** sound. Some of these are now so small they are no bigger than a grain of rice. They can be hidden in a pen, under a tablecloth, or behind a picture. They can be switched on and off from a mile away.

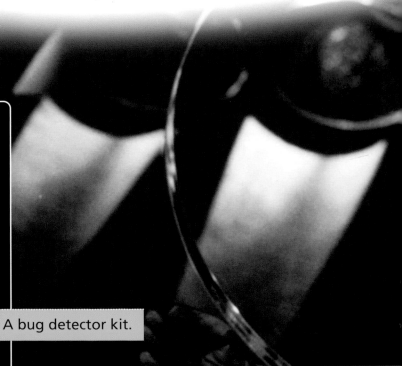

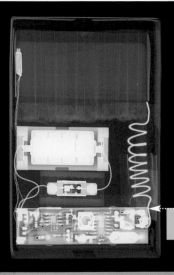

A bug detector kit.

Word Bank   **bugged** planted with a hidden listening device
detector equipment that senses what is near by

Taking a peek

Sometimes listening to a secret meeting is not enough. You might want to see what is going on. No problem – the spy kit has just the thing. Cameras have never been smaller. A lens can be as small as the head of a screw. In fact, the cameras can be made to look just like screw heads so they would not look out of place in any room. A light switch could easily hide a camera. It can transmit high quality colour images even in the dark. Those images can then be **enhanced** on a computer and the smallest details can be seen, even writing.

Can you believe it?

In 1945, the government of the **USSR** gave the US **Embassy** in Moscow a large wooden piece of art. It hung over the main desk where secret meetings were held. Seven years later they found it was bugged! Not to be outdone, the United States planted a bug in a Soviet military base. It was made to look like a tree stump just outside a window!

Planting bugs is dangerous work!

enhance improve, make clearer
transmit send out radio or television signals

Gadgets

Spies have been known to use all kinds of strange equipment. Often the tools of their trade are disguised so well that no one guesses what they might be used for.

How can you take pictures of the enemy's headquarters without being seen? If you want to break in, you will need a plan of the building. But how do you get this? Tiny flying cameras can now be made the size of real flies. They simply hover over the target and take pictures. Spies with flies! These are not so useful, though, on a windy day or with hungry bats about!

Playing your cards right

A spy on a **mission** may need to carry a map. But being found with a map by the enemy could be a give away. In the Second World War, spies often carried a pack of playing cards. Only when the top layer was peeled off could the hidden map underneath be seen.

Bugs can be disguised in all kinds of things, including dung!

Word Bank   mission   special task or job

Don't touch

The best way to stop anyone touching a spying device is to make it look like animal droppings! In the Cold War, secret agents needed to know when and where bombs were being tested. So they scattered dung on the ground. At least, it looked like dung. It was made to pick up signals. Agents could then measure movement in Earth's surface caused by the bombs going off.

No one would think twice about seeing a fish swim by a boat. But the **CIA** built a robot fish for moving close to boats of enemy agents. The fish was bugged and even carried a bomb – just in case!

A bird's-eye view

In 2004, the CIA put many of its spying gadgets on display for the first time. One trick the spies tried was fixing a tiny camera around a pigeon's neck. When the bird flew up to window ledges, it was easy for spies to see what was going on in different rooms!

The CIA's gadgets.

Codes

Spies are in the business of sending secrets. A message must never fall into the wrong hands. But if it does, it is important that the enemy cannot understand it. Without the key to a code, no one should be able to make sense of it.

An ancient way of sending a secret message was to wind a long thin strip of paper in a spiral around a stick. The message was then written on the paper in a straight line down the length of the stick. When the paper was unwound, the letters were all jumbled. To **decode** the message, someone just had to know what size stick to wrap it around before reading it!

Puzzle

In the Second World War, the Germans used special **enigma** machines to turn all their secret messages into code. No one would be able to crack the code ... or so they thought. Thousands of code-breakers in the UK worked on the coded messages. At last they cracked the code and the information they learned helped them win the War.

The enigma machine.

decode understand a code, turn it back into normal language
enigma mystery, or difficult to understand

Copying the code

Most codes need special books or computer programs to decode them. Breaking into the enemy offices to copy their code book needs great skill. If they know you have seen it, they will change the code. Some spies had to use their memories. They would stare at a page and try to remember it. It is much easier now with a tiny camera that fits in a ring on the finger.

Microdot cameras were first tried during the Second World War. A microdot is a tiny photo that can be hidden on a full stop. Then a whole page of code can be shrunk to 1/400th of its original size.

Hiding codes

Spies have found all sorts of places to hide their coded messages, in case they were caught. Microdots have been hidden inside shirt buttons. Coins have been hollowed out for hiding coded messages. Some spies have even had a tooth drilled so they can hide a message inside.

This microdot camera was first used in the 1940s.

Some spies hid secrets in their teeth!

microdot tiny photo of a message, shrunk to the size of a full stop

Secret weapons

When a spy is arrested, he or she will be searched. So gadgets and secrets need to be well hidden. If a weapon is disguised, it can be used before anyone knows what it is. Surprise is often the best way to attack.

Secret agents have always used secret weapons. One of them looks like a normal tube of lipstick. It is called "The Kiss of Death" and it can easily kill. A 4.5 millimetre (0.18 inch) single-shot pistol is hidden inside the lipstick. During the Cold War, other objects were also used to hide secret weapons. Torches, pens, tobacco pipes, and cigarette packets were actually guns in disguise.

This tiny pistol makes no noise when fired.

Silent but deadly

In the 1930s the **CIA** gave their spies small "silent" pistols. The head of the CIA fired one inside the **White House**. He shot ten bullets into a bag of sand then put the smoking-hot weapon on the desk to show President Franklin D. Roosevelt. The president was on the phone and did not hear a single shot!

Georgi Markov

inject force fluid into the body, usually for medical reasons

The deadly umbrella

Georgi Markov worked in London in the 1970s. Someone back home in Bulgaria wanted him out of the way. It may have been the **KGB** who killed him. Their secret weapon was unusual – it was an umbrella.

In 1978 Markov was waiting for a bus on Waterloo Bridge. He saw a man approach him with an umbrella, before he felt a jab in his leg. Three days later he died. Doctors found he had been **injected** with a deadly poison. The spy who killed him has never been caught.

Georgi Markov was attacked on this bridge.

Quite a kick
In the film *From Russia With Love*, James Bond had to cope with a Russian spy called Rosa Klebb. She had a secret weapon in her shoe. A poisoned blade shot out of the toe. With a quick kick, she was deadly. Maybe the killers of Georgi Markov got their idea from the world of make-believe spies.

White House house and office of the president of the United States

Spies and fiction

The spy of all spies

The first Bond book, *Casino Royale*, was published in 1953. In it, James Bond was already in his late thirties. If James Bond had really lived, he would be an old man of over 90 by now.

Casino Royale was the first Bond story.

More often than not, spying is theft. It can be dangerous and people get killed. It is a crime. Yet books and films love the world of **espionage**. It seems to be full of excitement.

007

James Bond, 007, is the best-known spy hero of all. Bond works for **MI6**, the British Secret Service, where his boss is simply called "M". Every Bond story has its **villains**. They often want to take over the world. So 007 has to destroy their plans and usually the villains, too. He has a **licence** to kill.

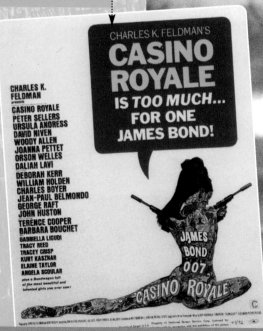

Word Bank   007 code number for the made-up spy James Bond
licence special permission, allowed to do something

The birth of a hero

Ian Fleming was the creator of the James Bond stories. He began to write his stories soon after the Second World War at his home in Jamaica. His spy would be cool. He would like gambling and fast cars. But what could he be called? Fleming looked at all the books on his shelf. He saw a bird book by a writer called James Bond. Perfect! So the spy was born, and became so popular that the stories were made into films.

In every Bond film, you can always bet on 007 escaping danger at the very last minute. He gets the girl, kills the villain, and saves the world. What a hero!

Bond is back...

Bond movies have kept going for over 40 years. All of Ian Fleming's stories were used up long ago but new writers keep giving 007 new plots to solve. The 20th film came out in 2002, with an old favourite *Casino Royale* as the 21st in 2006.

James Bond is the ultimate spy!

---

villain criminal or evil character in a story

Spies take great risks in the *Mission Impossible* films.

Mission Impossible

Spies on the big screen must cope with many scary **missions**. The action and music get faster as the danger increases! *Mission Impossible* films are famous for the music and for featuring spies in disguise. They often peel off a face mask to reveal their true identity!

In the first *Mission Impossible* film it is up to Ethan Hunt, played by Tom Cruise, to take on a spying mission. He has to find a secret list of spies, as well as discover who killed the rest of his team. Cruise also plays the hero spy in *Mission Impossible* 2 and 3. Real spies take big risks. Film spies take big money!

Teen spies

Books and films about teenage spies have always been popular. The heroes often stumble on secrets and warn the police, but no one believes them. The only answer is to tackle the **villains** single-handed and save the world.

Since the first *Spy Kids* film in 2001, teen spy films have become even more popular. The name Cody Banks was soon known in many countries. In *Agent Cody Banks 2: Destination London*, the hero has to spy in a London school to uncover an agent who stole a top-secret mind-control device. Would Cody stop the agent turning the world's leaders into **zombies**? Just a normal day's work for a teenage spy!

Fantastic fiction

Meet the junior James Bond of the 21st century. Teenage **fiction** now has another hero with a secret mission. Alex Rider is the boy caught up in the dangerous world of **MI6** and **espionage**. Fans enjoy reading about Alex's adventures in these popular spy books by Anthony Horowitz.

The *Spy Kids* films make spying seem very exciting!

And finally ...

We never really know the truth. Spying is a world of secrets and cover-ups. Spy **fiction** is often very far-fetched and nothing like the real world.

We can be sure that **espionage** has always gone on, and always will. Individuals use espionage to steal secrets to sell, or to get to the truth. Governments use it to find out what other countries are planning. Police use it to get evidence. Apart from usually being a crime, spying also helps to fight crime. Spying is a big part of today's world. It is all around us.

Who knows?

Computers store a lot of data about each of us. They record everything from our exam results to medical details. They know where, when, and how we spend our money. It only needs a spy to download files and our secrets are out! Protecting data is now a huge business and it is here to stay.

This satellite is being launched into space.

Word Bank   CCTV close-circuit television. CCTV cameras are in most shops and high streets.

You are being watched

Would you like to live in a country where you are always being watched? Perhaps you already do! The average person walking through a city will be filmed many times. **CCTV** cameras now record people in many towns and cities.

Even in the middle of a desert you can be seen. You may not see it, but a spy could be there. Satellites high in the sky are keeping watch on the Earth. Powerful cameras can photograph details on the ground. They can read a crossword from 200 kilometres (124 miles) up in the sky! If you thought spying was just fiction … it may be more real than you think.

The police are watching – to try to prevent crime.

A safer world?

With growing Internet **fraud** and terrorist threats, the security services are always listening, watching, and recording. Some people worry about losing their rights. It seems nothing can be really **private** any more. But being spied on is the price we now have to pay to be safe. Spying may actually make the world safer.

Find out more

How about this for a spy car?

James Bond's Aston Martin V12 Vanquish in *Die Another Day*.

A few extras...
- four mounted rockets with two machine guns
- two motion-sensing guns hidden under the bonnet
- spiked tyres for ice driving.

And at the flick a switch... the car can become invisible!

If you want to find out more about the criminal underworld, why not have a look at these books:

Behind the Scenes: Solving a Crime,
   Peter Mellet (Heinemann Library, 1999)
Forensic Files: Investigating Murders,
   Paul Dowswell (Heinemann Library, 2004)
Forensic Files: Investigating Thefts and Heists,
   Alex Woolf (Heinemann Library, 2004)
Just the Facts: Cyber Crime,
   Neil McIntosh (Heinemann Library, 2002)

Did you know?

- "Big Bird" was the popular name for the US spy satellite. First launched in 1971, "Big Bird" had two cameras that could photograph objects as small as 20 centimetres (8 inches) from a height of 200 kilometres (124 miles). This was the first US satellite that could photograph such small objects.

- Spy dust is a harmless powder the KGB used in the 1980s. The powder was sprayed on door handles, on floors, and in cars to trace the movements of US officials. The powder had no ill effects.

- An L-Pill was the name for a lethal or poison pill carried by spies. It was to be used as a last resort to escape **torture** that could make them reveal secrets. During the Second World War, some L-pills had a glass shell. Hidden in a false tooth, one could be bitten and the spy would die straight away. If the pill broke loose while the spy was sleeping, it would pass through the body without causing any harm.

Goldeneye

Q is the inventor of secret gadgets in the James Bond films. He shows Bond the secrets of a car:

Q: Behind the headlights are stinger missiles.

James Bond: Excellent. Just the thing for unwinding after a rough day at the office.

Q: Need I remind you, **007**, that you have a licence to kill, not to break the traffic laws.

Glossary

007 code number for the made-up spy James Bond

Al-Qaeda terrorist organization linked with attacks on New York and Washington D.C. on September 11, 2001

betray to act against your friend or country

bugged planted with a hidden listening device

CCTV close-circuit television. CCTV cameras are in most shops and high streets.

CIA Central Intelligence Agency of the United States

civil war when soldiers from the same country fight against each other

con artist someone who tricks people to get money

contact someone you know who has important information in business or government

convicted prove guilty of a crime

decode understand a code, turn it back into normal language

defence to do with a country's military organizations

detector equipment that senses what is near by

embassy office of a particular country inside another, foreign country

enhance improve, make clearer

enigma mystery, or difficult to understand

espionage spying to get secret information

executed put to death for breaking the law

expose show or tell everyone

FBI United States's Federal Bureau of Investigation

fiction not real – stories that are made-up

fraud deceiving another person

hacker someone skilled with computers who breaks security

identity person's name and individual details

illegal against the law

informer person who tells information

inject force fluid into the body, usually for medical reasons

intelligence secret information gathered by spies, which tells one country what another is doing

invade disturb or move in on

KGB secret service organization of Russia

legally allowed by law

licence special permission, allowed to do something

MI5 UK's military Intelligence unit 5

MI6 UK's secret service organization

microdot tiny photo of a message, shrunk to the size of a full stop

mission special task or job

mistrust having no trust in someone

Nazis government in Germany from 1933 to 1945 led by Adolf Hitler

nuclear to do with the reaction that happens when an atom is split

peasant poor country person who works on the land

phone tapping listening in on a telephone call

political beliefs about power and how to organize society

privacy freedom from being disturbed or watched

psychiatrist doctor who deals with the mind, feelings, and behaviour

regret sadness or disappointment about what has happened

revenge get even with someone

rival enemy or competitor

rumour story that may not be true

SOS cry for help: Save Our Souls

spymaster person in charge of a network of spies

stalker someone who watches and follows other people

surveillance watching closely

torture causing great physical and/or mental pain to get information

traitor someone who betrays another person's trust – or their own country

transmit send out radio or television signals

treason crime of harming your country, or of helping its enemies during war

undercover acting in secret inside an organization

USSR Union of Soviet Socialist Republics – now called Russia

vault room or compartment for storage or safe keeping

villain criminal or evil character in a story

White House house and office of the president of the United States

zombie someone in a trance, as if they have no mind of their own

Index